The Off Grid Guide to Field Medicine

By: Tristan Trouble

Published in USA by:

CDI Publications, LLC
P.O BOX #9
Boynton Beach
FL 33425

ISBN-13: 978-1718709478
ISBN-10: 1718709471

Table of Contents

Introduction

One of the most troubling aspects of developing a survival strategy is trying to figure out what to do about the medical category. There are quite a few options available to us. Getting a first aid kit should be a top priority. This first aid kit should contain as much medical gear as possible. Stocking up on and storing OTC (Over-The-Counter) and prescription drugs and medications would also be a great idea.

Researching and developing alternative means for

tending to our healthcare should also be part of the process. Essential Oils and herbal remedies are sure to come in handy for long term survival situations and should be something we add to our emergency preparedness kits. Most of us already know this and have planned to obtain these items. Off grid medical guides, such as the one here, are also something we should have available to us should we ever have to go off grid for any length of time.

This Off Grid Guide to Field Medicine addresses several issues we could all find ourselves facing in a grid down scenario. The information and material contained within this guide has been assembled to address injuries more commonly associated with those seen on a battlefield. As preppers we hope we never have to deal with serious injuries of this sort; however, we also realize that the odds of experiencing an injury of this magnitude, or being tasked with attending to the injured, are significantly increased. Therefore, we must ensure we are fully prepared to handle any type of event when we are off grid, for it is then that we are most assuredly responsible for ourselves.

One of the threats that preppers are most concerned

with today is that of civil unrest, and possibly even war. America has several enemies on the international scene, not to mention politically motivated riots, mass shootings, and the ever present threat of government overreach in the form of rights' infringement, which has many people suggesting we may need to fight to preserve our rights if we want to keep them for future generations. These are but a few of the more recognizable threats that we face as US citizens, and any one of them could erupt into a nightmare on the national scene at any time.

Should America ever find itself in the position of dealing with massive unrest, foreign invasion (although unlikely, it is a possibility), or unacceptable government overreach, any of which result in a national disaster, there is a good chance hospitals will either be overrun, or incapable of offering much assistance due to employee evacuation and/or the absence of grid supplied power. Even if traditional hospitals are operational, it may be entirely impossible to reach them in time to save a life.

Although this material focuses on injuries of an extreme nature, much of the caregiving advice offered can be applied to less serious injuries that are commonly suffered during survival situations. Readers are advised to seek hands on education for practicing the techniques outlined in this guide as it is not intended to be a step-by-step instructional manual.

Purpose of This Material

The information presented in this guide is intended to serve the reader as a reference only resource for performing various first aid techniques and tending to extreme injuries. As stated previously, readers are encouraged to consider taking hands-on classes, such as CPR, First Aid, Search & Rescue, etc., to receive proper training on performing the procedures mentioned in this guide.

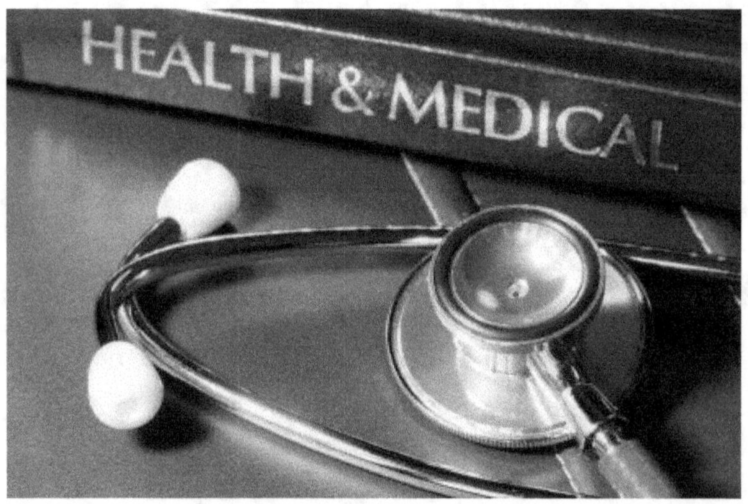

Although medical attention may be administered using this reference guide, further treatment from qualified medical personnel may also be necessary. This guide is intended to assist the reader with performing first aid tasks, stabilizing the situation as quickly as possible, and preparing the injured party for transport to an environment better suited for providing continued care. This guide contains information for performing first aid as a solo operation, as well as using the buddy system. It does not however cover surgical procedures that are commonly performed in trauma/triage centers or conventional hospitals by qualified medical staff.

Off grid medical training is something every member of the family, and/or prepper group, should be well-versed in, provided they are of age. The more people in your group who are trained to provide field level first aid, the better prepared the entire group will be for handling life threatening situations when they occur.

The advantage of learning first aid has many advantages, especially in an off grid environment. Not all injuries, accidents, and events are going to be of the minimal nature, where basic first aid will suffice to save the day. The actions we take immediately following such a situation could be the difference between saving a life and having to bury a member of the group. These procedures should only be considered if a more educated medic/doctor is unavailable to provide immediate attention to the injured, and the injury suffered is of a serious nature, such as stopping massive blood loss, dealing with compound fractures, amputations, partial amputations, and chest decompression, just to name a few.

Lifesaver's EDC Gear

All individuals within your group who have been through first aid training should be tasked as primary caregivers for the party. As such, they should have a medical EDC (Every Day Carry) kit on them at all times. This kit should be easy to retrieve and use.

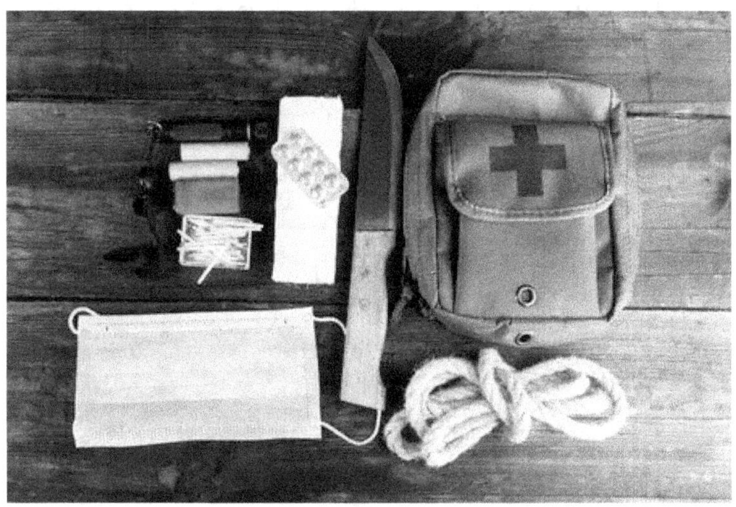

Any gear contained within the EDC that is used in the field must be replaced as soon as possible upon return to civilization; this will prevent being unprepared for future injuries and accidents. Additionally, any medical equipment that is not disposable should be cleaned and sterilized before being returned to the kit for future use.

In extremely dire situations, it may be necessary to send a runner back to base camp for additional supplies, or to retrieve additional personnel to help transport the injured back to a safer environment. This should only be done if doing so will improve the odds of saving the injured. In the event a runner needs to be sent, consider using the buddy system to reduce the odds of a single runner getting lost along the way and also needing rescue; again, this should only be done if there are enough members to do so. Never leave an injured party alone to retrieve additional supplies or help; consider establishing a signal fire to alert those back at base camp.

Tactical Off Grid Care

Tactical Off Grid Care refers to medical procedures that must be conducted in a disaster zone; the injured party must receive care on site before they can be transported to a safer environment. It could also refer to providing medical treatment in a combat zone. Although military combat zones do not currently exist within the borders of the US, mass shooting events and terrorist attacks are occurring with greater frequency, and they can replicate an environment similar to those found in combat zones. Although prolonged gunfights and battles are not necessarily part of these events, they very well could be at future events, so we must be prepared for them at all times; as such, this guide will cover providing medical care under these conditions.

When a traumatic injury occurs that requires immediate medical attention, death becomes a real possibility if treatment cannot be administered on site. The odds of a fatality occurring can be greatly reduced with proper first aid, buddy aid, and trauma/triage training. Most deaths associated with disaster and combat zones are a direct result of massive hemorrhaging.

In the event medical treatment of an injured person occurs under fire, the primary objective should be to return fire first; attending to the wounded is put off until it is safe to do so. If the injured party is able to move, they should be given instructions to seek cover and wait for further assistance. Under no circumstances should a caregiver enter the line of fire to retrieve an injured person; an injured person may be used by the assailant to attract additional targets into the field of fire, which could ultimately result in more fatalities. When under fire, survival should focus on oneself first, the injured and others second. Although this may sound harsh, it prevents the group from suffering greater loss.

Three Phases of Treatment:

> **Under Fire-refers** to an environment where gun battles, bombs, etc., are present and being used. The first order of business is to find cover and determine in which direction to return fire. Medical attention is seriously limited under these conditions. If possible, use verbal commands to determine the severity of wounds received by the injured. Primary

treatment in such an environment often consists of applying a tourniquet to prevent massive hemorrhaging. Further care is only administered once the injured has been relocated to a safer environment.

- ➢ **In the Field-refers** to the environment just outside the disaster/combat zone. This area is considered somewhat safer than being under direct fire; however, this environment could change rapidly if the disaster/combat zone expands. Medical equipment and care in such an environment remains restricted and should consist of minimal lifesaving techniques.

- ➢ **Evacuation & Relocation-**refers to removing the injured party from the disaster/combat zone to a much safer location here further medical treatment can be provided. Off grid caregivers should accompany any injured personnel to the evacuation area if the wound is of a grave nature and additional medical personnel are unavailable. However, if the wound has been properly stabilized and additional medical personnel are available to accompany the injured, then the off grid caregiver should remain on scene to assist with treating any other injured personnel and ensure they are transported to safety.

Under Fire

This section refers to situations in which the caregiver and injured personnel are in an environment that is active; a shooter is still loose and on the rampage, a bomb has detonated, etc. When under these conditions, there are certain actions that should be taken first, followed by further actions when possible.

The first actions to take, referred to below as "primary actions," are those that must be taken before injured personnel can receive treatment. These actions should not be skipped or excluded for any reason when in an active environment; they are designed to keep the caregiver safe and to reduce further injury to the fallen.

Primary Actions:

> **Find Cover** - cover refers to things which are capable of stopping a bullet completely; a building, a vehicle, a concrete wall, etc. This is not the same as concealment which only serves to hide your position from others, but it incapable of stopping a bullet.

> **Return Fire** - if the environment remains active and you have the means, return fire in the direction of the subjects committing the act; with any luck you will hit one or more of the culprits which could bring the situation to an end, or drastically reduce the effectiveness of those who initiated the attack.

> **Suppressive Fire** - if possible, lay down suppressive fire on the location of the culprits committing the act; this may allow innocent bystanders the opportunity to vacate the area.

> **Injury Identification** - if possible, ask the wounded personnel to describe and detail the extent of their injuries. This will help you determine the seriousness of the situation and develop a plan of action for moving forward.

> **Determine Patient Mobility** - if the injured patient is still able to move, direct them to seek cover and wait further instructions.

> ➤ **Relay Information -** when possible, tell others of the situation so the information can be relayed to medical personnel who may be waiting outside the active environment; this will allow them to prepare for the arrival of the injured and develop plans for providing medical treatment.

Secondary Actions

Although referred to as "secondary actions," these steps should be implemented prior to retrieving or attending an injured person within an active environment.

> ➤ **Inspect Area -** before moving towards an injured person to provide care or evacuate, check the area for signs of danger; are active shooters still present, are people still escaping the area in unorganized fashion, are bombs still detonating, are buildings or vehicles on fire, etc.
> ➤ **Inspect Adjacent Area -** take a look around the immediate area and try to identify a suitable structure to use as cover; this needs to be an area where injured parties can be transported easily. When possible, the area chosen should be as close as possible to the place where the injured person is waiting; transportation of an injured individual can cause further damage so the less they are moved, the better.
> ➤ **Plan Retreat Route -** once a suitable location for evacuation has been chosen, you must plan the route of retreat/escape. Use as much cover and concealment as possible when retrieving the injured

as well as when transporting them to the safe location. Plan the route to the injured, as well as from the injured to the location for safety, before you initiate the retrieval of the patient.

➢ **Call In Cover Fire -** if necessary, request cover fire from all able bodies while retrieval of the patient is performed; this will help prevent the evacuation party from coming under fire while they have their hands full with an injured and possibly immobile patient.

➢ **Injury Anticipation -** consider the environment and the action taking place when trying to anticipate the types and severities of possible injuries. Were they hit by small arms fire? Were they incapacitated by an explosive device? Were they hit by falling debris, or did they fall from a significant height? Try and determine what type of care will be necessary. Will you be addressing gunshot wounds, broken bones, and/or partial or full amputations? Be ready to apply the proper techniques.

➢ **Additional Device Usage -** if possible, use additional devices to your advantage when retrieving or evacuating an injured person. Additional devices could include smoke grenades, Molotov cocktails, etc. The purpose of this is two-fold; it may provide additional concealment for the responding parties, and/or it may create a distraction that draws the attention of the culprits in a different direction.

Actions Upon Arrival

This section refers to those actions the medical caregiver will take upon arriving at the location of the injured personnel. These are not actions that can be accomplished from a distance regardless of the information received from the injured personnel prior to caregivers arriving on scene.

- ➢ **Immediate Assessment & Evaluation** - upon arrival at the location of the injured an immediate assessment & evaluation of the injuries should be accomplished. Determine what care can be provided under the current conditions and location, and what care should be reserved until after the patient has been evacuated to a safer location.
- ➢ **Prioritize Patients** - if the situation consists of more than one injured person, then the assessment should prioritize which patients require the most assistance, or more serious assistance to prevent loss of life.
- ➢ **Check Vital Signs** - determine how responsive the patient is first; are they alert and aware of their surroundings, or are they dazed, confused, and discombobulated? Are they unconscious, if so check for signs of life; are they breathing, is there a pulse?
- ➢ **Provide Treatment** - treat the injured according to how they have been prioritized. This must be adhered to in order to provide the best chance of survival for the most people. Without patient prioritization, the odds of maximizing the survival rate are significantly reduced.

Procedures & Performance

This section provides a step-by-step guideline for

performing basic first aid procedures to injured patients. It will also cover several methods of evacuation that may be used to transport the victims to a safer environment for further medical assessment or treatment. As mentioned previously, hands-on training for these procedures is strongly recommended.

- ➤ **Check Responsiveness** - the purpose of this procedure is to determine the cognitive condition of the patient; are they responsive, unresponsive, alert, aware, confused, exhibiting abnormal behavior, in shock, etc. This will allow the caregiver to develop better plans of action for handling the situation.
  - o Verbally ask if they are alright. Check for audible and visual responses; they may be able to speak, or they may only be able to give a sign, such as a "thumbs up."
  - o Unresponsive patients should be tapped/lightly shaken to check for a response.
  - o Responsive patients should be asked for additional information, such as location and severity of injuries, as well as the level of pain/discomfort. This will help the caregiver determine and develop an appropriate plan of action.
  - o Apply cognitive questioning to responsive patients; name, date of birth, day of the week, geographic location, etc. This will inform the caregiver as to the mental awareness of the patient and help determine

the accuracy of the information provided by the patient regarding the location and severity of their injuries and pain thresholds.

- Shock is a very real possibility under these conditions. Patients in shock may be unaware they are even injured. Shock is also a good indicator that the injuries/wounds are more problematic than the patient thinks.

o Use the AVPU scale when making determinations regarding levels of awareness and responsiveness.

- A-Alert. The patient gives sound logical replies to all questions being asked.
- V-Verbal. The patient responds to verbal commands yet does not reply audibly. (Example: They nod their head to respond or can give a hand gesture).
- P-Pain. The patient is not alert and does not respond to verbal commands, yet when touched near the injury/wound they make sound, or display movement indicating the sensation of feeling pain.
- U-Unconscious. This does not necessarily mean they are dead, simply unresponsive to all forms of determining consciousness. They may still be alive. Check for other signs of life, pulse and breathing.

- ➢ **Control Bleeding & Stabilize -** these procedures should be done prior to transporting an injured person to a safer environment for further treatment.
    - o Inspect the injured for signs of blood loss with a focus on massive arterial bleeding first.
    - o Apply a tourniquet if necessary and available, make a tourniquet is necessary and unavailable. The tourniquet should be applied over the clothing between the injury and the patient's heart.
    - o If the patient has a partial or full amputation, apply the tourniquet immediately, even if massive blood loss is not yet apparent. When the body goes into shock from enormous trauma it defends itself naturally, shutting down blood supply temporarily to the injured area. Massive hemorrhaging will eventually be evident with this type of wound.
    - o If the area is still considered "active," then apply the tourniquet immediately and evacuate the injured patient to a safer location before performing pressure dressings or other procedures for stopping blood loss.

Evacuation Methods

This section provides various methods for evacuating an injured patient from an "active" disaster zone to a safer location for further medical treatment. When possible, injured patients should try to assist as much as possible with their evacuation. This will increase the odds of everyone making it to safety while reducing the burden on those who have arrived to help them evacuate. Injured patients will not always be able to provide evacuation assistance, which is where the methods listed below will come in handy.

- ➢ **Dragging** - there are several methods of dragging an injured person to safety. Dragging provides a rapid retreat method that is most effective over short distances.
- ➢ **One Man Drag** - this method requires a single person to retrieve the injured. This is done by grabbing the clothing, a strap, or a piece of gear with one hand and dragging the injured to a safer location. The person retrieving the injured should keep their eyes trained towards any threats in the area. The retriever must be prepared to release the injured long enough to handle any threats that may be hampering the retrieval. Dragging with this method is often done while walking backwards.
- ➢ **Two Man Drag -** this method is similar to the one man drag but calls for two people to retrieve the injured. Each person will grab clothing, gear, or a strap on opposite sides of the injured and drag them to safety. This is a much faster method than the one man drag; however, it does increase exposure which may not be favorable under certain conditions.
- ➢ **Cradle Dragging** - similar to the one man drag, this method calls for the person retrieving the injured to grab them beneath the armpits from

behind and drag them to a safer location. This is a bit quicker than performing the one man drag.

In addition to the dragging methods mentioned above, there are several methods of carrying an injured person to safety. Carrying is different than dragging as the individual retrieving the injured must shoulder some, or all, of the weight of the victim.

- ➢ **One Man Support** - this is the basic 'shoulder crutch" method where the injured is helped to their feet and supported by placing an arm over the shoulder of the person helping them to safety. This method is only used if the injured is able to assist with the process of getting to a safer location.
- ➢ **Two Man Support** - is the same as the one man support listed above only it calls for two people to act as rescuers and shoulder crutches for the injured. This may be a quicker method of retrieving an injured person and getting them to safety.
- ➢ **Two Man Gurney** - this method calls for two people to retrieve the injured by grabbing and lifting them horizontally from the feet and armpits respectively. The people performing the retrieval can walk facing each other or facing the same direction.

Tactical In Field Care

Tactical in field care refers to treatment provided to the injured by the caregiver when all parties have been relocated to a safer location, yet not in an actual medical facility. The treatments provided at this stage are intended to stabilize the injured for transportation to a conventional medical facility if available.

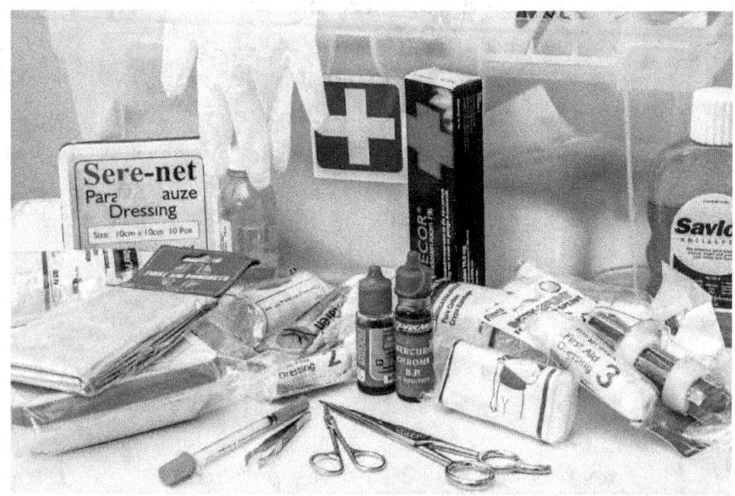

> **Tourniquet Reassessment -** if you applied a tourniquet prior to evacuating the injured to a safer location, then now is the time to reassess the application and make any adjustments if necessary.

- o **Exposure** - expose the wound and determine if the tourniquet is really necessary; the injury may not be as bad as originally thought.
- o **Application** - if the tourniquet is deemed necessary, then apply a new tourniquet. Place this tourniquet on the skin rather than the outside of the clothing. The tourniquet should be placed 2-4" above the wound.
- o **Removal & Dressings** - if the tourniquet is deemed unnecessary, then use other methods to control blood loss, such as pressure dressings, direct pressure, blood clotting agents, and/or elevating the injury above the heart.
- ➤ **Check for Wounds** - once the injured party has been transported to a safer location, inspect the rest of their body thoroughly to identify additional wounds that may require treatment before they are transported to a medical facility.
- ➤ **Evaluation & Treatment** - in addition to checking for additional wounds, the caregiver should also continue to evaluate conditions and provide treatments for the injured. These areas of interest may or may not be visible.
  - o **Airway** - check for and remove any obstructions if possible; maintain a clear airway at all times.
  - o **Chest Wounds** - cannot be treated with a tourniquet. The caregiver needs to be familiar with pressure dressings, clotting agents, etc.
  - o **Fractures** - check for and identify any fractured bones; splint them if necessary and

possible without causing further injury. Caregivers should not attempt to reset any fractures as this could cause additional injury.

- o **Pain Treatment** - if pain is present and medication is available, then administer per instructions of the medication.
- o **Shock** - identify and treat the injured for shock if necessary and possible.

➢ **Communication** - this is an extremely important part of the process. All members of the party should be kept abreast of the situation with the injured. This information will assist the group with making decisions regarding what actions to take next. It may be necessary to send two or more members to seek additional help, or it may be necessary to develop an evacuation schedule that calls for rotating the duty of transporting the injured.

- o **Additional Assistance** - if someone in the group has better medical knowledge and experience, then they should be tasked with assessing the injured and determining the care to be given on site. If this individual has been tasked with performing other duties, those duties should be doled out to the other members of the party so that the medically experienced individual is always available to help the wounded.

➢ **Monitoring** - the caregiver in charge should continue to monitor the injured periodically until such a time as they have been transported to a medical facility for further treatment.

- o **Consciousness** - use the AVPU scale mentioned previously to reassess the injured person's level of consciousness. This should be repeated until the injured appears to be alert and cognizant.

- o **Chest Decompression-**if the injured person has an open chest wound, or exhibits difficulty with breathing, they need to be transported to a medical facility as soon as possible.
- o **Document Changes-**if the condition of the injured improves or declines, make note of it and share this information with all involved. This information should accompany the injured to the medical facility when they are transported.

➢ **Evacuation Preparation -** prior to the injured being moved to a medical facility for further treatment, there are a few things to be considered.

- o **Records-**using whatever means and methods are available, document everything identified as an injury/wound, as well as any treatments/actions/ procedures implemented. This information needs to be attached to the injured so that the medical staff receiving the injured knows what has taken place. This information may be vitally important to the survival of the injured party.
- o **Request Evacuation-**if possible request evacuation services. In certain circumstances it may be necessary for the primary caregiver to accompany the injured to the medical facility. If the primary caregiver cannot accompany the injured, then a member of the evacuation party must have enough

medical knowledge to monitor vital signs during evacuation and transportation.

Examination & Application Techniques

This section will cover several of the concepts included with providing care to an injured person. These are activities that will likely be performed in a very stressful environment. Many of these actions will take place at the site of the injury, or in close proximity, prior to transporting the patient or evacuating them to a medical facility.

Positioning the Injured

If the injured person has a head, neck, or spinal injury, then do not move them as this could cause further damage. Attempt to make the injured as comfortable as possible and await the arrival of qualified medical personnel with proper equipment to perform the recovery procedure.

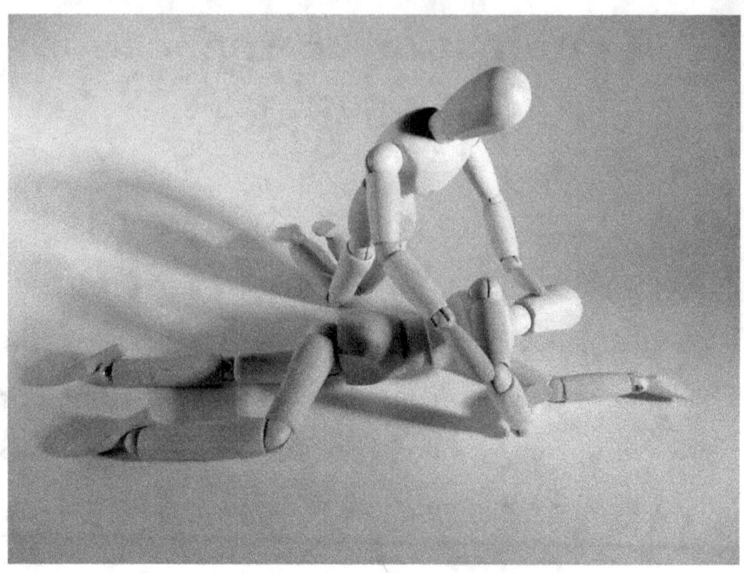

In the event the injured party does not have a head, neck, or spinal injury, then consider moving the injured into the "recovery position," as shown in the image above.

> **Kneel -** down next to the injured on one side of the body, knees touching soil near the shoulders of the injured about to be turned over.
> **Grab -** the arm opposite you and place it above the injured person's head
> **Place -** the legs of the injured next to each other and lay them flat.
> **Place -** one hand on the head and neck area of the injured.
> **Grab-**the nearest shoulder of the injured and prepare to rotate the body away from you.

> ➤ **Rotate-**the injured person slowly and steadily, keeping their head and neck in line with the body.
> ➤ **Place-**the arm of the individual in the bent position as shown in the image above and move the upper leg to the position as in the picture above.

Check Breathing

If the wounded person is alert and breathing on their own, then simply continue monitoring their condition periodically. The purpose of the monitoring is to assure their condition doesn't change for the worse and the breathing doesn't become more difficult. If the breathing is labored or difficult, then take the following actions.

> ➤ **Tilt Head/Lift Chin-**this is the standard method taught in CPR classes. This is the first method of checking for breathing that should be applied. If the airway is blocked by the injured person's tongue, this method should free the airway.
> ➤ **Look, Listen, & Feel-**once you have performed the Head Tilt/Chin Lift method, kneel down beside the wounded, put your ear next to their oral and nasal passages. **Look** at their chest for signs of breathing; the rise and fall of the chest cavity. **Listen** for breathing sounds; the inhale and exhale of air and **Feel** for actions of breathing on the side of your face, or the back of your hand.
> ➤ **CPR/Rescue Breathing-**if the individual is not breathing, then perform CPR techniques, or the rescue breathing portion of them if chest

compressions are not possible due to complications with injuries.

- ➤ **NPA (Nasopharyngeal Airway)** - there are two situations when a caregiver should insert one of these mechanisms to assist with breathing; if the injured person is breathing on their own, yet remains unconscious, or if the injured person is conscious yet their breathing is troubled, difficult or sporadic. *Do not attempt to introduce one of these devices without proper training!*
- ✓ **Recovery Position-**after you have completed inspection of the injured and have determined no further complications or injuries, roll them on their side into the recovery position, which was described above. *(Note: This position will allow any buildup of excess fluids, such as mucous and/or blood, to continue draining from the oral cavity, keeping the airway as clear as possible).*

Inspect for Fractures

As soon as possible inspect the injured person for fractured bones. A few of the signs to look for are listed below.

- ➤ **Fragmentation-**refers to broken bones that can be seen penetrating the surface of the skin.
- ➤ **Swelling & Bruising-**will often appear in the immediate area of a fractured bone but may also be the result of a serious sprain, so inspect carefully.
- ➤ **Deformity-**a fractured limb may also appear to be deformed yet show no signs of bone penetrating through the skin area.

- ➤ **Immobility-**the injured person may have difficulty, or be completely incapable of moving the fractured limb, or portion of the limb containing the fracture.
- ➤ **Massive Injury Visible-**if a massive injury exists it may be masking all or part of the signs and indications of a fracture previously mentioned. All evidence may suggest nothing more than a wound, yet a fractured bone could still be present and undetectable until blood loss has been controlled and further inspection can be performed.
- ➤ **Snapping Sound Reported-**in some cases the injured person may report hearing a snapping sound. If so, assume a fracture exists and proceed accordingly to determine the evidence and make decisions on treatment.
- ➤ **Splint Application-**if a fracture is discovered, then properly splinting the fractured limb will alleviate pain and stabilize the region until further surgical treatment (setting of the bone) can be completed. To fashion a splint, you will need two rigid objects and several strips of cloth.

Leg Splint

This section offers guidance for applying a leg splint. In the event a leg splint needs to be applied some of the materials mentioned may need to be substituted with whatever makeshift arrangements are available until the injured can be seen by a medical professional for further treatment.

- ➢ **Securing Straps-**take the strips of cloth and slide them beneath the flexible bend of the knee. Slide them up or down the leg from this position to intervals appropriate for securing. *(Note: Do not place a securing strap directly over the fractured area as this could increase pain and decrease circulation).*
- ➢ **Above & Below-**if/when possible, place two of the securing straps above the site of the fracture, and two below the site of the fracture. Additional straps should be placed above and below any moveable joints, such as the knee or ankle.
- ➢ **Pole Placement-**these are the rigid objects used to make the splint. These need to be placed beside the fracture in such a way they immobilize any joints above and below the fracture area. For instance, if the fracture is in the lower leg, the splint poles should extend above the knee and below the ankle. If the fracture is in the upper leg, then the poles should extend above the hip, (at least on the outer side), and below the knee.
- ➢ **Padding-**insert additional padding between the splint poles and all areas of the limb it is applied to. Additional padding may also be necessary for painful areas, such as joints and knees. Refrain from using too much padding as this could create too much pressure and reduce circulation.
- ➢ **Wrapping the Straps -** wrap the securing straps around the fractured leg so that the splint immobilizes the area of interest.
- ➢ **Tie the Tails-**tie off the ends of the securing straps where they meet. These straps and knots should be tied off against the poles themselves and not come into contact with the fractured limb. Make sure to tie them off on the outer side of the splint poles,

this will make accessing and re-securing procedures easier to accommodate.

> **Inspect Circulation-**once the splint is in place inspect the fractured limb for circulation problems. If you notice any signs of poor circulation, such as numbness to the affected area, a noticeable difference in body temperature to the fractured limb, or you cannot detect a pulse in the fractured limb, then loosen the securing straps and retie them. *(Note: The securing straps should be just tight enough to ensure the splint and fractured limb remain immobile, yet loose enough to allow blood to circulate through the region).*

> **Evacuation-**the injured person should be evacuated as soon as possible for additional medical treatment and surgical procedures.

Arm Splint

This section offers guidance for applying an arm splint. In the event a arm splint needs to be applied some of the materials mentioned may need to be substituted with whatever makeshift arrangements are available until the injured can be seen by a medical professional for further treatment.

> **Pole Placement-**the splint poles should be placed on opposite sides of the fractured arm. If/when possible these poles should extend above and below associated joints. For instance, in a lower arm fracture, the poles should extend above the elbow and below the wrist. For an upper arm fracture, one

pole should extend above the shoulder, and both should extend below the elbow.

- ➢ **Padding-**stuff padding in between the splint poles and the fractured limb. Again, use just enough to stabilize the situation without increasing pain or reducing circulation.
- ➢ **Securing Straps-**the same principle applies here as for leg splints. Two above and below the fracture, as well as above and below the joints to be immobilized.
- ➢ **Inspect Circulation-**this is the same as for leg splints. Loosen and retie securing straps if necessary to accommodate for circulation.
- ➢ **Slings-**if/when possible, apply a sling to the fractured arm and splint. This will help immobilize the arm.
- ➢ **Swathes-**for upper arm fractures apply swathes to help immobilize the fractured area.

Identifying Shock

Shock is a very real possibility when a serious injury occurs. Shock is a part of the body's natural defense mechanisms and usually occurs when patients experience serious trauma.

- ➢ **Hypovolemic Shock-**this normally occurs when a traumatic injury is experienced. There are several things that can result in hypovolemic shock; massive blood loss, 2nd or 3rd degree burns, and internal bleeding just to name a few. *(Note: Internal bleeding is* *not something that can be properly addressed or treated under the conditions being described. Do what you can and try to have the individual evacuated as soon as possible).*

➢ **Signs & Symptoms**-there are several indications that can be recognized and assessed as warning signs that shock is present.
  o **Sweating**-if present will be cold and clammy to the touch
  o **Skin Color**-patients may exhibit a change in color to the skin, becoming paler during the process
  o **Blue Hue**-patients in shock may also exhibit a bluish hue around the mouth area.
  o **Nausea**-patients may experience nausea. This does not always refer to vomiting but it may include it.
  o **Anxiety**-patients may become restless, nervous, and or agitated.
  o **Cognitive Consciousness**-patients may pass out or appear confused and disoriented. Consciousness should be checked and monitored every 15-20 minutes. Patients may be fine at one examination and completely incoherent moments later.
  o **Rapid Breathing**-patients may begin to hyperventilate, gasping or gulping for air.
  o **Dry Mouth**-patients may exhibit dry mouth conditions, or insist they require more hydration.

➢ **Treating Shock Patients**-it isn't necessary for the caregiver to witness signs of shock before attempting to treat the individual exhibiting the signs. Shock treatment procedures are also effective means for preventing shock in the first place. One should always assume that shock is present within an injured patient until such a time as it can be determined that shock is no longer present.

- o **Positioning**-place the injured person in the shock treatment position. The shock treatment position is flat on the back with both feet elevate slightly above the heart. This is intended to improve circulation procedures.
- o **Ground Protection**-place a poncho, blanket, or other insulating material between the patient and the ground. This will offer some comfort and climate control for the injured person's body.
- o **Body Temperature-**keep a close eye on the injured. Ensure they do not overheat or become too cold. Make necessary adjustments if necessary.
- o **Restrictive Clothing-**loosen but do not remove all tight fitting garments and outwear, boots included. This will help improve circulation.
- o **Reassurance-**patients need to be reassured that the situation is under control and that the caregiver is doing everything they can to improve their condition. Refrain from discussing serious injuries or wounds in front of the individual as this could increase anxiety, rather than keep them calm.
- o **Request Additional Help-**if someone in the group has more medical experience, or better medical equipment, send for them. If you must go after help yourself, turn the injured person's head slightly, explain to

them to keep that position while you are away, and tell them you will return with help. *(Note: The head should be turned and kept in this configuration in order to prevent suffocation should vomiting occur).*

- o **Minimal Hydration-**if the individual is conscious allow them to have small sips of water.
- o **Evacuation-**if/when possible, evacuate the injured to a better and safer medical environment for further treatment.

Shock Treatment Exceptions

In certain circumstances it may be necessary to avoid placing an injured person in the shock treatment position described above. Some injuries and conditions will be too severe for the injured person to be placed in such a position without risking further injury or damage.

- ➢ **Unconscious Individuals-**injured people that remain unconscious should be placed in the recovery position detailed previously. If an unconscious individual vomits, clear the obstructions from the airway using a finger sweep.
- ➢ **Spinal Fractures-**individuals suffering from a fracture to the spinal column should be placed on their back. Do not elevate the feet! Stabilize and immobilize as much of the head, neck and spinal column as possible.

- **Open Abdominal Wounds-**individuals suffering from these types of wounds should be placed flat on their backs. Bend and flex the knees, placing the feet on the ground so the knees stay flexed. This will reduce discomfort and pain to the abdominal cavity.
- **Open Chest Wounds-**individuals suffering from these types of injuries should be placed in the sitting position against a stationary support; wall, tree, vehicle, or whatever is readily available. If a stationary support structure is unavailable, place the injured in the recovery position, injured side towards to the ground. This will allow the uninjured lung to function easier and should reduce pressure to the uninjured area.
- **Minor Head Injuries-**individuals suffering minor head injuries should also be placed in the seated position against a stationary support structure. If such a structure is unavailable, then place them in the recovery position, ensuring the injured side of the head remains up.

Additional Concerns for Shock Treatment

- **Lower Limb Splints-**if the patient requires a splint to be applied to a lower appendage, then do not elevate the feet until the splint has been properly put in place and secured.
- **Temperature Control-**patients being treated in warm climates should be kept in the shade. If natural shade is unavailable, manufacture it. In cold climates the patient should be kept warm. Use a space blanket or additional methods to ensure they maintain core body temperature.

- > **Fanning-**use hand fans to reduce and dry perspiration if necessary.
- > **Body Temperature-**even in extremely warm weather a patient suffering massive blood loss will exhibit abnormally cool body temperatures, be cognizant of this fact and be prepared to respond accordingly.
- > **Tourniquets-**if the patient has one or more tourniquets do not cover them to the point they will not be easily recognizable upon evacuation to a better medical facility.
- > **Chemical Containment-**if the injured person is in an area where chemical agents have been used, refrain from loosening any exterior garments as this could result in chemical infections of the wound areas.

Evacuation Procedures

If/when possible injured persons should be evacuated to a safer location for further medical treatment and care. In a survival situation this may not always be possible. When and where it is possible, there are a few things to keep in mind regarding the movement of injured personnel.

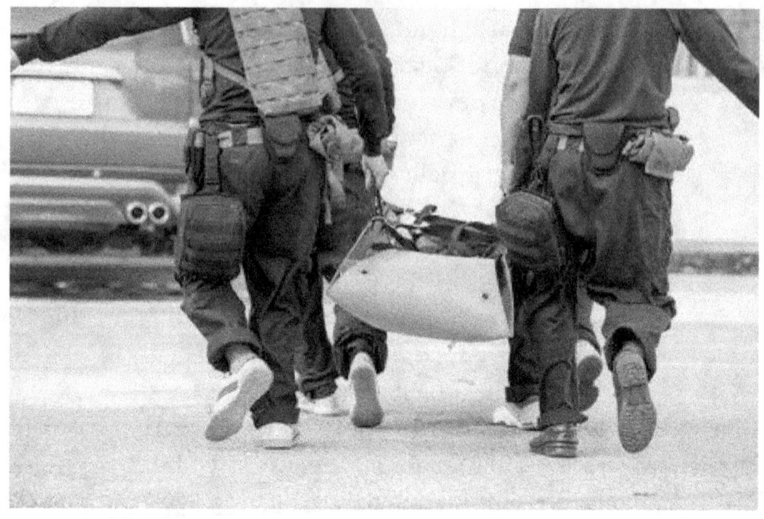

> **Prepare a Litter--**this is a 2-4 man operation that requires the use of a gurney or stretcher; fabricate one if necessary. The injured should be placed on the litter in the same position they were in while medical techniques were applied in the field.

> **Monitor & Share Info-**if the injured is to be moved and the in-field caregiver is not going to accompany the litter, then make sure all procedures have been documented and passed on with the patient. Assign a caretaker to monitor the injured individual during transportation.

> **Evacuating Amputees-**if the injured person has suffered a full amputation, then ensure the amputated appendage is transported with the individual. If possible rinse and remove all debris from the amputated appendage. Wrap the amputated limb in gauze. Rewrap in plastic and place in a container to keep cool. **Do Not:**

- o freeze the amputated appendage
- o place it in water
- o place it in direct contact with ice or refrigerated devices
- o place it on dry ice
- o place it where the injured individual can see it

➢ **Caregiver Positioning-**if the caregiver is available to assist in the evacuation, they should assume a position on the litter detail at the left shoulder of the patient. This will allow for easier monitoring during transportation.

➢ **Transportation of Litter-**regardless of whether you are using a 2 man or 4 man litter detail, the litter should be lifted in unison. Once lifted, the litter detail should walk in step to prevent bouncing the injured individual around.

Controlling Blood Loss

This section covers the proper methods of controlling blood loss. Massive blood loss can lead to fatality, especially when out in the wilderness where traditional medical procedures, equipment, and knowledge are unavailable. Stopping blood loss provides the injured with a better chance of surviving long enough to seek additional medical attention and treatment. If blood loss cannot be controlled effectively and quickly, the injured patient will more than likely perish before adequate medical attention and treatment can be rendered.

- **With a Tourniquet -** a tourniquet is used to control/stop the loss of blood when applying bandages, direct pressure, and pressure dressings will not get the job done effectively. A tourniquet should be reserved as a last resort and must be applied properly to prevent further complications.
    - **Amputations -** if the injured patient suffers from a partial, or full amputation, then a tourniquet must be applied to control the loss of blood.
    - **Active Scene Application -** if/when the caregiver and patient are within an active scene (mass shooter/bomb detonation), a RAT (Rapidly Applied Tourniquet) should

be applied. This can be something as simple as a strip of cloth placed above the wound and tied securely. The primary focus in environments of this type should be to get in, stop the bleeding, and evacuate to a safer location.

- ➤ **Wound Exposure** - depending on the circumstances, the wound may need to remain covered, or it may need to be exposed, before proper care can be administered.
  - o **Active Scenes** - when the scene remains an active situation, the wound should never be exposed. Apply a tourniquet over the clothing, above the wound, and prepare the patient for immediate evacuation.
  - o **Inactive Scenes** - if the scene is no longer considered active, then the wound can be exposed before a tourniquet is applied. Cut away and remove clothing from the general vicinity using caution and care. Make sure clothing is the only thing being cut; do not increase the severity of the wound by nicking it. *(Note: If clothing appears stuck, or burned, onto or around the wound, do not remove this section of clothing, cut or rip around it and leave it attached to the injured area. If chemical agents are present or expected, do not remove the clothing, place any and all dressings, bandages and/or tourniquets over the clothing).*
- ➤ **Wound Inspections** - when possible, all wounds should be thoroughly inspected prior to treatment being rendered. Proper inspection of the wound(s) can reduce future complications and increase the possibility of proper treatment.

- **Checking the Body -** a complete and thorough examination of the injured person's body should be conducted if/when possible. Again, this is not a procedure to be done in an active scene; remove the injured person to safer ground prior to inspecting the body.

- **Bullet Wounds -** when inspecting the body for entry/exit wounds from bullets, it is important to understand that these projectiles can enter the body at one location and exit in an entirely different part of the body from where one might expect. Bullets can fragment and tumble as they pass through the body, so the caregiver must inspect the entire body, front, back and sides to identify wounds and treat them properly. *(Note: Depending on the type of projectile, exit wounds may be much larger than entry wounds, they will therefore usually require a heavier dressing/bandage).*

- **Buried Bullets -** if an entry wound is located but an exit wound is not, then assume the bullet remains lodged within the body of the patient. Do not attempt to remove a bullet until the injured has been transported to a controlled environment, such as a medical facility. Dress the entry wound and prepare the patient for evacuation.

- **Protruding Projectiles -** this refers to injuries where a sharp instrument/object remains lodged and protruding from the body of the patient. Do not attempt to remove the object; dress the wound with heavier bandages around the protrusion and prepare the patient for evacuation.

➢ **Emergency Bandage Application** - although all members of the group should be trained in basic first aid and off grid medical procedures, the person designated as the primary caregiver should carry and EDC kit that has more medical gear than the others; bandages and wound dressings are disposable, so they are not suitable for reuse.

  o **Gloves** - if/when possible, the caregiver should use sterile medical grade gloves as a protective measure against contamination from blood borne pathogens.

  o **Dressings** - such as gauze pads should be applied directly to the wounded area(s).

  o **Bandages** - should be applied over dressings to hold them in place.

  o **Securing in Place** - once bandages have been placed over the dressings, they must be secured in place to prevent further complications and contamination.

➢ **Combat Gauze** - is something we should all have in our off grid medical kits. Combat Gauze is a roll of gauze that contains a hemostatic agent. Combat Gauze promotes coagulation of blood upon contact and is often applied with direct pressure to stop arterial bleeding from serious injuries.

  o **Remove Clothing** - strip away clothing from the wound area with caution and care; remember to leave clothing that is stuck to the wound, or that has been burnt to the flesh, and apply dressings and bandages over it.

- o **Excess Blood -** should be rinsed away from the wound area while leaving any clotting in place.
- o **Identify & Prioritize -** find the area of the wound and locate the source resulting in the largest amount of blood loss.
- o **Apply Combat Gauze -** pack this material directly into the wound using pressure and wrap with additional combat gauze once the bleeding has stopped. *(Note: The patient may experience pain during this process, it is a necessary procedure, so ensure they are held stable and immobilized to prevent obstruction of the process).*
- o **Additional Gauze -** in certain situations it may be necessary to use more than one roll of combat gauze; use as much as needed to get the bleeding to stop.
- o **Repack & Adjust -** depending on the situation, it may also be necessary to repack the combat gauze and adjust the bandages holding it in place to stem the loss of blood.
- o **Direct Pressure -** should be applied for at least 3 minutes to control/stop/stem the loss of blood. If blood continues to flow, then use more combat gauze and continue to apply direct pressure. *(Note: If the individual is conscious and capable they can apply direct manual pressure, if not then the caregiver will have to perform this procedure).*
- o **Pressure Bandage -** should be applied over the combat gauze once bleeding has stopped to hold it firmly in place during evacuation.
- ➤ **Pressure Dressings -** should be applied to the wound if direct pressure does not stop the loss of

blood. This treatment should only be performed after the patient has been treated for shock and their feet have been elevated.

- o **Padding Placement -** once the wound has been dressed and bandaged, an improvised pressure bandage can be applied to help reduce or control blood loss. Fold up a piece of clean cloth material, (this does not necessarily have to come from the medical first aid kit, it can be a piece of scrap material since it will not be coming in direct contact with the wound itself), and place this over the gauze and bandage, directly over the wound area. Take an additional scarp piece of cloth and secure this in place as tight and firmly as possible. *(Note: Do not use wire or string material as the securing device unless nothing else is readily available as these instruments could cut off circulation and cause further damage).*
- o **Check Circulation -** check the injured person's body temperature in an area directly below the bandage; the area furthest from the heart. If the skin is cool to the touch, loosen the knot and retie the pressure bandage in place. Continue to check circulation periodically and adjust as needed.

➢ **Digital Pressure Techniques -** this is the application of direct pressure using fingers, thumbs, the heel of a hand, or the bend of a knee, to an accessible area of the human body where an artery is known to flow through. This method of applying direct pressure might help stop/reduce the flow of blood so that other procedures can be attempted or applied.

Tourniquet Applications

A tourniquet is a constrictive medical device designed for the specific purpose of stopping arterial blood flow. The tourniquet is a device intended to be used on an extremity, such as a leg or arm. It is not to be used for head/neck injuries or around the torso. Determining whether or not a tourniquet is required is of the utmost importance when assessing an injury.

> ➢ **Extremity Wounds -** if arterial bleeding is present in an extremity, such as the thigh, lower leg, upper arm, or forearm, and pressure dressings have been applied in conjunction with direct pressure, yet the dressings remain soaked with blood, or blood loss has not stopped, then apply a tourniquet. *(Note: If a patient is suffering from multiple injuries where arterial bleeding is present, the procedures followed may be inefficient for stopping all blood loss. If there are more than one injured person(s) requiring medical attention, prioritize the patients according to severity and address those with a greater chance of surviving their injuries).*
>
> ➢ **Amputees -** if a patient is suffering from an amputated limb, partial or full, then a tourniquet is required. This applies to all amputees, even if massive blood loss is not present at the time of assessment and initial treatment. Do not assume that the lack of blood flow from an amputated limb indicates a controlled situation. *(Note: In situations*

where the patient and caregiver are in an active environment, or where and when time does not permit additional assessment and medical treatment, a RAT (Rapidly Applied Tourniquet) is the recommended procedure. Additionally, if you are unable to control bleeding by any other means, such as pressure bandages, direct pressure and dressings, then use a tourniquet. It is always better to sacrifice a limb than to sacrifice the life, use the tourniquet!).

➢ **CAT Application** - the CAT (Combat Applied Tourniquet) is a medical device designed specifically for military battlefield environments. If you do not have a CAT in your medical prepper kit, then you should consider getting one as soon as possible. These tourniquets are designed for rapid application under stressful situations and in active environments.

  o **Single Handed Application** - all members of the prepper group should have a CAT in their kits at all times. They should also have the skills to perform a single handed application of the CAT; this will allow an injured, yet conscious person the ability to attend to their own wound(s) if the caregiver is not available.

    ▪ Remove the CAT from packaging
    ▪ Insert the wounded appendage through the loop created by the CAT
    ▪ Slide the CAT to a position on the appendage that is 2" above the wound site.
    ▪ Tighten the securing strap and attach it back onto itself.

- Wrap the CAT band around the injured limb. (Note: Do not wrap this strap over or beyond the red colored locking clip).
- Twist the tightening rod of the CAT until such a time as the arterial bleeding ceases. (Note: Dark red blood may continue to seep or drain from the wounded area for a brief period of time once the CAT is properly in place and tightened).
- Insert the twisting rod into the locking clip and secure firmly in place.
- Check the wounded appendage for signs of continued blood loss or a pulse. If either is present below the CAT, retighten and secure the twisting rod again.
- Wrap the end of the CAT securing strap around the rod, through the clip and over the entire limb.
- Make sure the CAT rod securing strap and CAT band are secured in place and continue checking the patient and extremity periodically, making any necessary adjustments required.

- **Two Handed Application -** this technique is generally used for arterial bleeding injuries occurring to a leg. The leg being a larger limb than the arm, more pressure is required to stop the flow of blood. The two handed application technique provides the measures necessary to accomplish the additional pressure required. When using this method, the friction buckle of the CAT is implemented, which is not standard for the single handed application techniques mentioned above.

- Remove the CAT from its packaging.
- Place the CAT band 2" above the wound area of the injured limb.
- Slip the red tip of the CAT band through the inner slot of the friction buckle. Pull tight.
- Slip the red tip of the CAT band through the outer slot of the friction buckle. Pull tight.
- Pull the CAT band tight and firm, then secure the CAT band back on itself.
- Twist the tightening rod with both hands until the arterial bleeding has ceased.
- Insert the tightening rod into the locking clip and secure in place.
- Check the injury periodically and frequently for signs of continued blood loss and make any necessary adjustments as required.
  - If arterial bleeding is present, or if such bleeding resumes, then apply a second CAT above the first CAT. Do NOT remove the 1st CAT!

- - Reexamine the injury to ensure the arterial bleeding has stopped.
  - If the application of 2 CAT's does not stop or control the bleeding further medical assistance is required ASAP!

➤ **Improvised Tourniquet Applications** - in the event a CAT is unavailable, an improvised version of it can be fabricated by gathering a few materials. Improvised tourniquets can be fabricated from almost any type of pliable cloth material, such as a roll of gauze, muslin bandaging, or even a torn shirt. It will also require a makeshift tightening rod, something that can be twisted/turned, and withstand the force applied during such activity.

  o **Gather Materials** - use a 3' X 3' piece of cloth, cut diagonally to form 2 separate and equal triangles. Lay the triangle out, top facing away from you. Grab the top tip and fold down to the bottom edge. Grab the top fold created by the previous action and fold down to the bottom edge. Repeat this step once again for a third fold. You should now have a tourniquet band that is 2" wide and will retain its shape when tightened. *(Note: A belt, the long sleeve of a shirt, or other wide strap, can also be used as the tourniquet band if time does not permit for the rapid fabricating of a cloth tourniquet band).*

  o **Tightening Rod** - use rigid material to form the rod. This could be a stout and sturdy wooden stick broken off a tree, about the thickness of a broom handle. It should be long enough to extend through the tourniquet bands and be grabbed by both hands on opposite sides of the band itself.

- o **Additional Binding Material** - cut additional strips of cloth to use as securing straps for the improvised tourniquet.
- o **Site Selection** - the improvised tourniquet is applied to the injured limb 2"-4" above the site of the wound/amputation. *(Note: If the first improvised tourniquet does not completely cease the flow of blood, a second improvised tourniquet should be applied 2"-4" above the first improvised tourniquet. Do not remove the first improvised tourniquet).*
- o **Improvised Application** - this is how the improvised tourniquet is applied.
    - Wrap the improvised tourniquet band around the selected site.
    - Secure improvised tourniquet band with a half knot. (A half knot is created by completing the first half of tying a shoe).
    - Set the tightening rod on top of the half knot, vertically and centered.
    - Secure the tightening rod in place with a square knot. (A square knot is created by completing (2) half knots).
    - Turn the tightening rod (clockwise/counterclockwise). Continue tightening until such a time as the bright red (arterial) bleeding has stopped. (Note: Dark red blood comes from veins, not

arteries, and may continue to flow even if the improvised tourniquet has been applied correctly).

- Check and monitor the injury for signs of pulse below the tourniquet band. If a pulse or bleeding persists, or is present, apply a second improvised tourniquet as described above.

- Secure the tightening rod in place with at least one additional strip of cloth by wrapping it around the injured limb, then tying off both ends of the strip to one end of the tightening rod. Make sure the tightening rod is secured firmly in place and cannot loosen itself.

- Mark date and time of tourniquet application on the injured person's skin in permanent marker. Tourniquets can be applied effectively and left in place for approximately two hours without creating additional concerns or complications. This information will alert any other attending medical staff of the conditions.

- Apply additional dressings to the wound/amputation. This will help prevent further injury and infection.

- Monitor the injured person and wound site periodically. Under no circumstances should a tourniquet be covered with other dressings. It should remain visible at all times, so it can be seen by any other attending medical personnel.

Airway Management Methods

Depending on the nature of the injury and environmental conditions, an injured person may experience difficulty breathing, or may not be able to breathe on their own. If this situation arises, it will be necessary to clear the airway and perform certain procedures in an attempt to restore breathing.

- **Seek Safety First -** breathing restoration techniques should be done in a safe environment. If the injured patient is in an active environment, they should be moved to safety as fast as possible before any rescue breathing techniques are administered.
- **Use AVPU Scale -** this has been described in a previous section of this guide and should be employed to determine the injured patient's level of consciousness, responsiveness, and cognitive abilities.
- **Positioning the Patient -** this has also been previously described in this guide as the "recovery position." This is the position the patient should be placed in.
- **Open Airway -** use the standard head tilt/chin lift method to open the airway. Even if the patient appears conscious and breathing, this position can assist with maintaining airflow.
  - Kneel next to the patient's shoulder.

- o Place the palm of the closest hand on the forehead of the patient. Apply firm but gentle pressure in a backwards direction, tilting the head.
- o Using the other hand, place the tips of the fingers below the jawline along the chin and lift the chin in a forward direction.
- o If necessary, use the thumb of the chin hand to gently depress the lower lip and keep the mouth open.
- o Inspect the oral cavity for obstructive material; dentures, broken teeth, bile, mucous, blood, bone fragments or vomit. If any type of foreign substance is identified use the finger sweep method to clear the obstruction from the airway.

➢ **Check Breathing** - lower an ear towards the patient's oral and nasal passages while visually inspecting the chest cavity; look, listen, and feel for signs of breathing.

➢ **Determining Techniques** - after checking for sings of breathing, the next step involves deciding what actions to take next.

- o If the patient is breathing on their own, and is conscious and responsive, then monitor respiratory rate for a period of at least 15 seconds. If the patient exhibits less than two full respirations within the 15 second time frame, then insert an NPA (Nasopharyngeal Airway) if available. (Note: This is an item that may need to be purchased separately if current First Aid and medical gear do not contain them). Place the patient in the Recovery Position.

- o For patients who are breathing on their own, are conscious and responsive, yet have a guttural/snoring noise associated with their breathing, insert the NPA and set patient in Recovery Position.
- o For unconscious/unresponsive patients, insert NPA and use the Recovery Position.
- o For patients that are not breathing on their own, and who do not have an open chest wound, check for a pulse along the carotid artery. If a pulse is identified begin performing CPR/rescue breathing techniques.
- o For patients who are not breathing, or attempting to breathe on their own, and who have an open chest wound present, treatment is unlikely to produce favorable results. If there are more than one wounded, treat others with clear vital signs first.

➤ **Rescue Breathing Techniques -** these techniques should only be attempted if there are no other injured people, or if those injured people are being properly attended to by someone with sufficient medical knowledge and equipment. With rescue breathing, the caregiver blows air through the injured person's mouth and into the lungs. The caregiver then allows the air to be expelled. This replicates the human body's natural breathing exercise.

- o Kneel next to the injured person near the shoulder area.
- o With the injured person in the head tilt/chin lift position, pinch the nasal passages closed.
- o Open your mouth and inhale deeply.

- o Keeping your mouth open wide, place yours over theirs, ensure a good seal is created and blow forcefully.
- o Attempt to visually inspect the injured person's chest cavity during the process. If air is making its way into the injured person's lungs the chest should rise.
- o Release your pinch on the nasal passages and allow air to expel. Visually inspect the chest area here as well; it should fall.
- o Evaluate the effects of the rescue breathing attempt. If the patient's chest rose and fell as expected, then continue the rescue breathing efforts, one breath for every 5 seconds. If the patient's chest did not rise and fall as expected, make sure the head tilt/chin lift position has not been compromised. Reexamine the airway for obstructive material and remove. Repeat initial rescue breathing attempt and reevaluate effects. If the chest rises and falls continue rescue breathing efforts, one breath every 5 seconds. If chest fails to rise and fall, discontinue efforts and attend to other injured individuals first.
- o Check the patient's carotid pulse every 60 seconds. Examine and inspect the injured person while performing this procedure to see if they have begun or are continuing to breathe on their own.

➢ **Checking Carotid Artery -** this technique will assist the caregiver with determining the presences of a pulse.

- Place the palm of your hand on the forehead of the patient to maintain a clear airway.
- Locate one of the carotid arteries. This can be done on either side of the patient's neck, use the side closest to your location. Feel for one on either side of the windpipe, where the groove is located.
- Using your first and second fingers of the hand that is free, find the artery and check for a pulse. Continue checking for 5-10 seconds.
- Evaluate and determine appropriate actions as needed.
- If a pulse is present, yet the patient is not breathing on their own, then continue rescue breathing efforts, checking the carotid artery every 60 seconds.
- If no pulse is present and the patient is not breathing on their own, CPR procedures can be implemented so long as all other concerns have been met, and all other patients have been attended to, otherwise rescue efforts should be ceased to maximize medical attention where it may be more effective at saving a life.
- If there is a pulse and the patient is capable of breathing on their own, evaluate and determine if an NPA insertion is required, or would assist with helping the patient breathe.
- Continue rescue breathing and CPR efforts as necessary, or until such a time they are deemed ineffective.

- ➢ **Inserting an NPA -** an NPA is a specially designed medical device. It may need to be purchased separately if not part of your First Aid Kit contents. This device is intended to be inserted through one of the patient's nasal passages to maintain an open airway while preventing the patient's tongue from falling/folding back on itself and blocking the throat. (Note: An NPA should not be inserted if the patient has had head trauma, has head trauma currently, the roof of the oral cavity is broken, or if there is brain matter visible from the patient's own head. An NPA should also not be used if there is the presence of clear fluid seeping from the ears or nasal passages of the patient as this could indicate a skull fracture).
  - o Place the patient on their back, face up.
  - o Lubricate the tubular end of the NPA with medical grade lubricant or water if nothing else is readily available.
  - o Using a thumb and forefinger grasp the tip of the patient's nose and tilt it up/back, exposing the nasal passage.
  - o Insert the tip of the NPA tube into the nasal passage.
  - o Rotate the NPA tube if necessary to align the pointed end with the inside dividing wall of the nose.
  - o Continue sliding/inserting the NPA until the flange of the device is resting against the nostril.
  - o Secure the NPA in place with a piece of tape, and instruct the patient to leave it alone, restrain their arms and hands if necessary. Otherwise place them in the

Recovery Position. *(Note: Do not force the NPA insertion procedure. If the NPA insertion is met with resistance or encounters an obstruction remove it from the current nasal passage and attempt the procedure in the patient's other nasal passage. If both are obstructed discontinue attempting to insert an NPA).*

➤ **Recovery Position** - the proper positioning for a patient being situated is the recovery position, which has been discussed previously in this guide.

Penetrating Chest Trauma Treatment

The human body has two lungs, each contained in its own airtight environment within the chest cavity. These airtight environments are under constant and consistent negative pressure when the body is operating/functioning normally. If the wall of the chest cavity is punctured, outside air could be allowed to enter the area. If the puncture is deep enough to penetrate/puncture one of these previously airtight environments, the lung within it will begin to collapse. It is possible for one or both airtight environments to be compromised from a single penetration/puncture wound. However, any compromise of either airtight environment will introduce interference with the patient being able to breathe. It will also reduce the quantity of oxygen available for the patient's body to use. In most cases the lung(s) will not collapse immediately, although it may seem as though they have, given the patient's response to the situation. They will however, continue to collapse as more outside air is introduced to the previous airtight environment. This creates a positive pressure condition and restricts, reduces, or prohibits the lung(s) from expanding as they would normally.

> - **Signs, Symptoms, and Signals of an Open Chest Wound** - there are a number of things that could cause a penetration of the chest cavity wall and airtight environment around the lungs, especially if the injured person was directly involved in an active environment and received injuries. Bullets, shrapnel, a knife blade, or other device could be the instrument causing the penetration/puncture wound. *(Note: When unsure if a chest wound has penetrated the airtight environment around the lungs, treat the wound as if it has).*
>   - Sucking/hissing sounds when the patient attempts to breathe are a good indication the airtight environment(s) has/have been penetrated.
>   - A patient that coughs up blood also exhibits signs of an open chest wound.
>   - A bubbly/frothy blood/air mixture is present in, or around the chest wound.
>   - Difficulty or distress while trying to breathe, rapid inhalations, gasping for air.
>   - Chest does not rise and fall normally.
>   - Increased sensation of pain in the chest or shoulder areas when the patient attempts to inhale.
>   - A bluish hue present in the oral area, including lips, tongue, and inner cheek linings, and/or in the fingertips, or the fingernail beds.

- o Signs indicating shock, such as a rapid or faint heartbeat.
- ➢ **Checking for Chest Wounds** - inspect the patient thoroughly, identifying all entry/exit wounds. If more than one penetrating/puncturing chest wound is present, attend to the first one you come across, unless the severity of another calls for immediate attention. Do not attempt to wash/rinse away blood, use your hands and fingers to search for and find wounds.
- ➢ **Exposing the Wound Area** - this area was covered previously but warrants repetition in this category. Cut, rip, or tear clothing away from the wound site, leaving any burnt or otherwise stuck fabric in place. If objects are still present, or protruding from the wound, do not attempt to remove them, apply dressings and bandages around and over the wound leaving the protrusion to be removed at a later time.
- ➢ **Sealing the Chest Wound** - in order to properly and effectively seal an open chest wound the use of nonporous material must be used; plastic, Saran wrap, cellophane, or something of a similar nature should be used. Gauze, bandages, and cloth fabric are breathable and will not suffice for sealing off an open chest wound. This nonporous material will stabilize the airtight environment until further surgery can be completed.
  - o Put on protective neoprene gloves if available, and time and conditions permit. This will reduce the chance of contamination from blood borne pathogens.
  - o Prepare the nonporous plastic patches. Each entry/exit wound will need its own plastic patch. These should be cut and fabricated to

extend 2" on all sides of the wound hole. These patches must also be able to lie flat against the skin of the patient, so make sure flexibility is a characteristic of the material being used.

o   Instruct the patient to exhale as much air as possible out of their chest cavity and to hold their breath as long as possible. The more air that can be expelled from the area, the better the patient should be able to breathe once the entry/exit wounds are properly sealed. *(Note: Conscious patients may resume normal breathing upon completion of the wound seal. If a patient is unconscious/unresponsive, wait for the chest area to deflate and time sealing the wound during this event, before the patient inhales again).*

o   Apply the plastic sealing patch directly over the wound. Inspect the positioning of the plastic patches ensuring a 2" minimum clearance is achieved from the all edges of the wound, reposition if necessary by sliding. Do not remove and reapply unless the original patch is insufficient in size and shape. Make sure none of the edges have been sucked inside the wound.

o   Secure the plastic in place over the wound, use medical grade tape, or wrap a roll of gauze or bandage around the entire torso and tie in place directly over the plastic seal patch.

o   Once the airtight patch has been secured in place, set the patient in the Recovery Position. If the patient is conscious and is able to breathe easier by sitting up, then allow them to do so, using a stationary back support to lean against.

Documentation

Documenting the injuries and procedures taken is of vital importance and for many reasons. Considering that this material is intended to be used as initial trauma care for a patient suffering a serious injury, possibly from within an active environment, documentation of events may have to be modified. A medical log of some sort should always be kept for the patient. This information should include, but is not limited to;

> - Name of Patient
> - Age (if known)
> - Date
> - Time
> - Type of Injury
> - Extent of Injury (Level of severity as determined by the onsite caregiver)
> - Treatment Procedures (detailed)
> - Vital Signs (Heart Rate/Pulse; Blood Pressure; etc., if taken and if possible)
> - Name of Caregiver

This information should be kept with the patient at all times, and if the patient is to be transported the documents should travel with them. Clear, concise, and legible writing should be applied to prevent confusion and complications with understanding and determining further action. If communications are available, include contact information for the caregiver so that future medical personnel may get ahold of them if necessary. This more than likely will not be possible, but if it is, make sure to include it. Use permanent marker when possible to prevent deterioration of the information contained in the document.

Conclusion

The material provided in this guide reflects emergency procedures to be performed by an individual with limited medical knowledge, education, and equipment. These are life saving techniques that have been designed and developed to utilize minimal procedures and equipment. In almost all cases the patient is going to need further medical attention and possibly even surgical procedures. Do not assume that the procedures performed in the field are the final solution. The environment in which these medical procedures are performed is extremely stressful and time is of the essence.

These medical procedures should be practiced using a variety of simulated scenarios without actually performing them unnecessarily. In other words, do not actually perform a chest needle compression technique on an *acting* patient, as this would obviously result in complications requiring a visit to the nearest hospital. Practicing these techniques will get you familiar with the generalized principles and procedures. However, classroom environments are seldom capable of replicating what a caregiver might come across in a real world setting.

The majority of the equipment mentioned in this guide is standard in military medical gear kits. These can be purchased online, as well as from a number of survival stores and outlets. These kits are commonly referred to as Combat Lifesaver Medical Equipment Sets. The equipment, instructions, and procedures listed here are also standard military battlefield applications. As such, the primary focus of this material is intended to guide the caregiver through the proper steps and procedures of attending to various injuries, stabilizing them, and preparing the patient to be evacuated for further treatment.

Considering that the majority of survival situations will involve very limited resources in the form of medical procedures, equipment, and personnel, additional treatment and care may not be readily available. The techniques described in this guide may help save a person's life initially; however, if further treatment is not obtainable, the life being saved could be temporary. It is highly recommended that as many people as possible within your survival group, be trained in a wide variety of off grid medical procedures.

Surgical solutions should only be performed by those with proper training. All members of the survival group, of relative age, should be properly trained in the various steps and procedures outlined in this guide.

Improvised litters can be fashioned out of a wide variety of unconventional equipment and should be used whenever possible for transporting an injured person. Litters distribute the weight of the injured patient better and allow for easier transportation techniques to be applied. Litters and stretchers can purchased and included in the survival gear, or they can be made from something as simple as two poles and a blanket, or two poles and a couple of jackets. Whenever possible do not move an injured person unnecessarily. Patient's suffering injuries should be immobilized as much as possible until such a time as they can be properly stabilized, treated, and deemed fit for movement. Evacuation will almost always be necessary and should be done in the safest manner possible.